Volume 1

AUNASTIE'S PINK RAINBOOTS

By Fola Arigbon

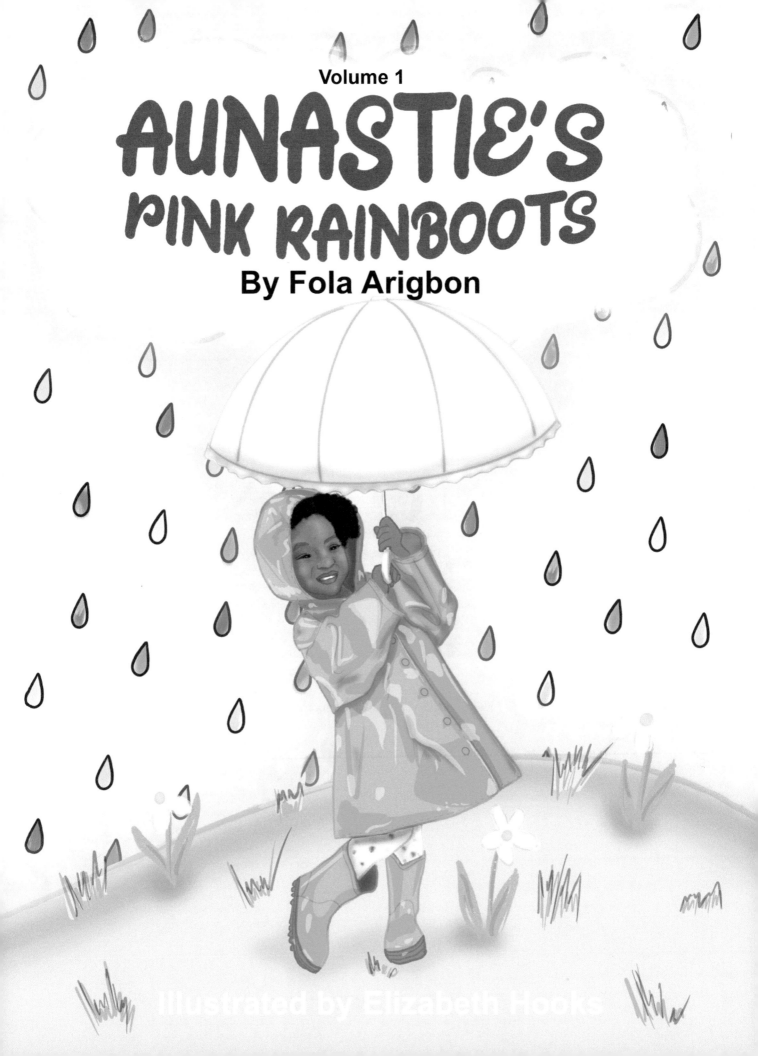

Illustrated by Elizabeth Hook

iUniverse books may be ordered through booksellers or by contacting:

iUniverse
1663 Liberty Drive
Bloomington, IN 47403
www.iuniverse.com
844-349-9409

Because of the dynamic nature of the Internet, any web addresses or links contained in this book may have changed since publication and may no longer be valid. The views expressed in this work are solely those of the author and do not necessarily reflect the views of the publisher, and the publisher hereby disclaims any responsibility for them.

Any people depicted in stock imagery provided by Getty Images are models, and such images are being used for illustrative purposes only. Certain stock imagery © Getty Images.

ISBN: 978-1-6632-2547-4 (sc)
ISBN: 978-1-6632-2548-1 (e)

Library of Congress Control Number: 2021913880

Print information available on the last page.

iUniverse rev. date: 07/12/2021

AUNASTIE'S PINK RAINBOOTS

By Fola Arigbon

Morning sunshine,
Wake up breakfast is ready and guess what?
you can wear your pink rain boots today.

Yes! I am so happy you're the best mom in the world.

Aunastie eat your breakfast, mommy needs to go to the grocery store before the weather gets too bad out today.

Ok mommy. I can't wait to wear my pink boots today it going to be so much fun!

Look at you Aunastie you're all soaking wet I'm glad you had fun today!!!!!!

Yes, I did mommy. Tomorrow can we do it all over again? Absolutely sunshine; Love you sunshine. Love you to mommy

Printed in the United States
by Baker & Taylor Publisher Services